CORPUS OF MAYA
HIEROGLYPHIC INSCRIPTIONS

**VOLUME 4   PART 1   ITZIMTE
PIXOY
TZUM**

CORPUS
OF
MAYA
HIEROGLYPHIC
INSCRIPTIONS

Volume 4   Part 1

ERIC VON EUW

Research Fellow
in Maya Hieroglyphics
Peabody Museum, Harvard University

PEABODY MUSEUM
OF ARCHÆOLOGY AND ETHNOLOGY
HARVARD UNIVERSITY
CAMBRIDGE, MASSACHUSETTS

1977

ACKNOWLEDGMENTS

The publication of this fascicle was made possible through the generosity of:

Mrs. Katherine Benedict

David D. Bolles

Members of the Cabot family, in tribute
to their grandfather, Dr. Samuel Cabot,
who experienced some celebrated
Incidents of Travel in Yucatan

Mrs. A. Murray Vaughan

Grateful acknowledgment is made to the Instituto Nacional de Antropología e Historia of Mexico for their cooperation in authorizing the necessary fieldwork in Yucatan, and for their permission to reproduce all the photographs in this volume. Fieldwork and preparation of the material published here were accomplished with support from the Stella and Charles Guttman Foundation of New York, and the National Endowment for the Humanities.

Itzimte-Bolonchen

LOCATION AND ACCESS

The ruins are located in a generally flat area surrounded by small hills approximately 2.5 km northeast of Bolonchen de Rejón, Campeche. The hills are often topped by structures of varying sizes, from low platforms to complex groups, some of which are visible on the eastern side of the Bolonchen-Uxmal highway.

Itzimte is readily accessible. A *milpa* road breaks off the main highway about 2.5 km from the center of Bolonchen, and the site is reached after a walk of about 500 m on this road.

There is an *aguada* in the site, but it is often waterless. The nine wells of Bolonchen are also unreliable sources of water in the dry season, but the Mexican government has now installed a potable water system in the town.

PRINCIPAL INVESTIGATIONS AT THE SITE

The first recorded visit to Itzimte was made by John Lloyd Stephens in 1842 (Stephens 1848, pp. 139-141). He spent only a short while at the site as even at that time it had been badly looted by the townspeople of Bolonchen who had carted away many of the facing stones. Consequently his description of the site was sketchy.

In 1887 Teobert Maler visited the site (Maler 1902, pp. 216-217) and, in somewhat more emotional terms than Stephens, decried the looting. In his report he included a photograph of the then still relatively well preserved Structure 58, which has since collapsed.

Neither Stephens nor Maler nor later reports (for example, Ruz Lhuillier 1945, p. 47) mention the existence of inscriptions at the site, although Stephens did run across the "headless trunk of a sculptured body" which has since disappeared.

Following a report of looting of ruins near Bolonchen, a preliminary visit to the site was made in March 1973, when the existence of sculptured stelae was ascertained. The recording of the sculpture and the mapping of the site were carried out later that year in two visits totaling 18 days.

NOTES ON THE RUINS

It is most unfortunate that so much stone has been taken from Itzimte. Not only has the removal of carefully cut facing stones detracted from the beauty of the structures, but in several cases it has resulted in their collapse. In many instances the structures have been so savagely bulldozed that their original shape can not be determined. And yet, despite over 140 years of stone removal, there are still impressive vestiges left.

Perhaps the most important group at the site is that formed by Structures 1 to 4, surrounding a raised plaza. Structure 1 is the largest in the group, rising to about 13 m above ground level (8.5 above plaza level) and is especially noteworthy because of the size of some of its rooms: one, for example, is 13.2 m long, 2.85 m wide, and 4.25 m high. In the well preserved room under the northern stairway there is a capstone decorated in low relief. Clear evidence of a painted hieroglyphic band can still be distinguished on the plaster covering the only wall of Structure 4 that still stands.

The other large group is formed by Structures 16 to 19, Structure 19 being the highest (height: 9 m).

There are many other dispersed structures in the site, several of which are built on hilltops. (Most nearby hilltops in fact have some evidence of construction.) Some are nothing more than flattened platforms containing in many cases one or more chultuns, but in other cases a more complex group of structures has been constructed on the hill: the group formed by Structures 35 to 37 surrounds a plaza 8.5 m above the foot of the hill.

The largest and most impressive structure in Itzimte (Structure 63) was also built to take advantage of the natural terrain. Only the front has been finished with artificial terraces, the back showing little more than the natural contour of the hill. A staircase leads to a platform 4.5 m high, on which there is a row of ten rooms, the central portion forming a part of the platform on which the pyramidal base for the highest structure rests. Structure 63,

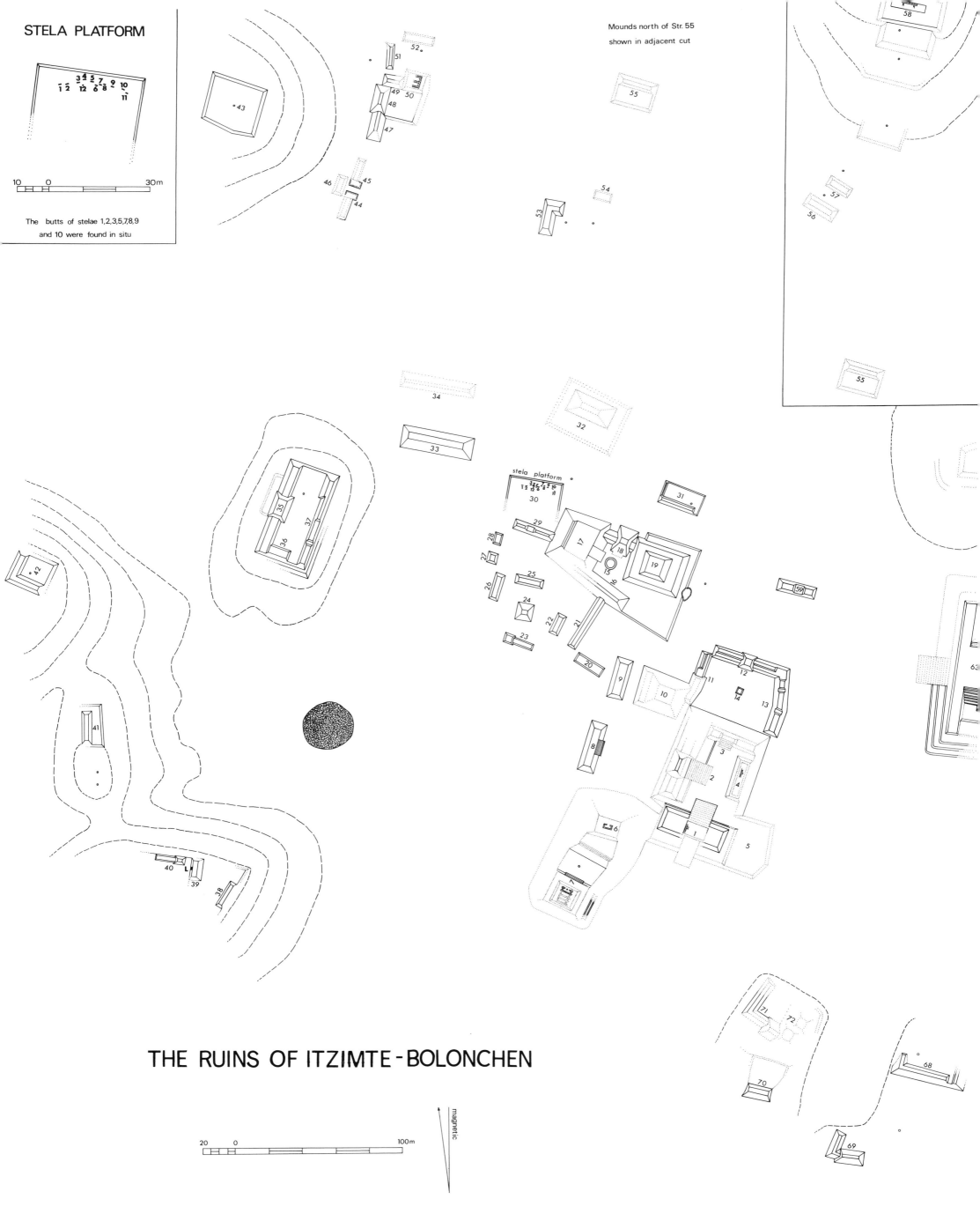

STELA PLATFORM

10   0   30m

The butts of stelae 1,2,3,5,7,8,9
and 10 were found in situ

Mounds north of Str. 55

shown in adjacent cut

magnetic

20   0   100m

THE RUINS OF ITZIMTE-BOLONCHEN

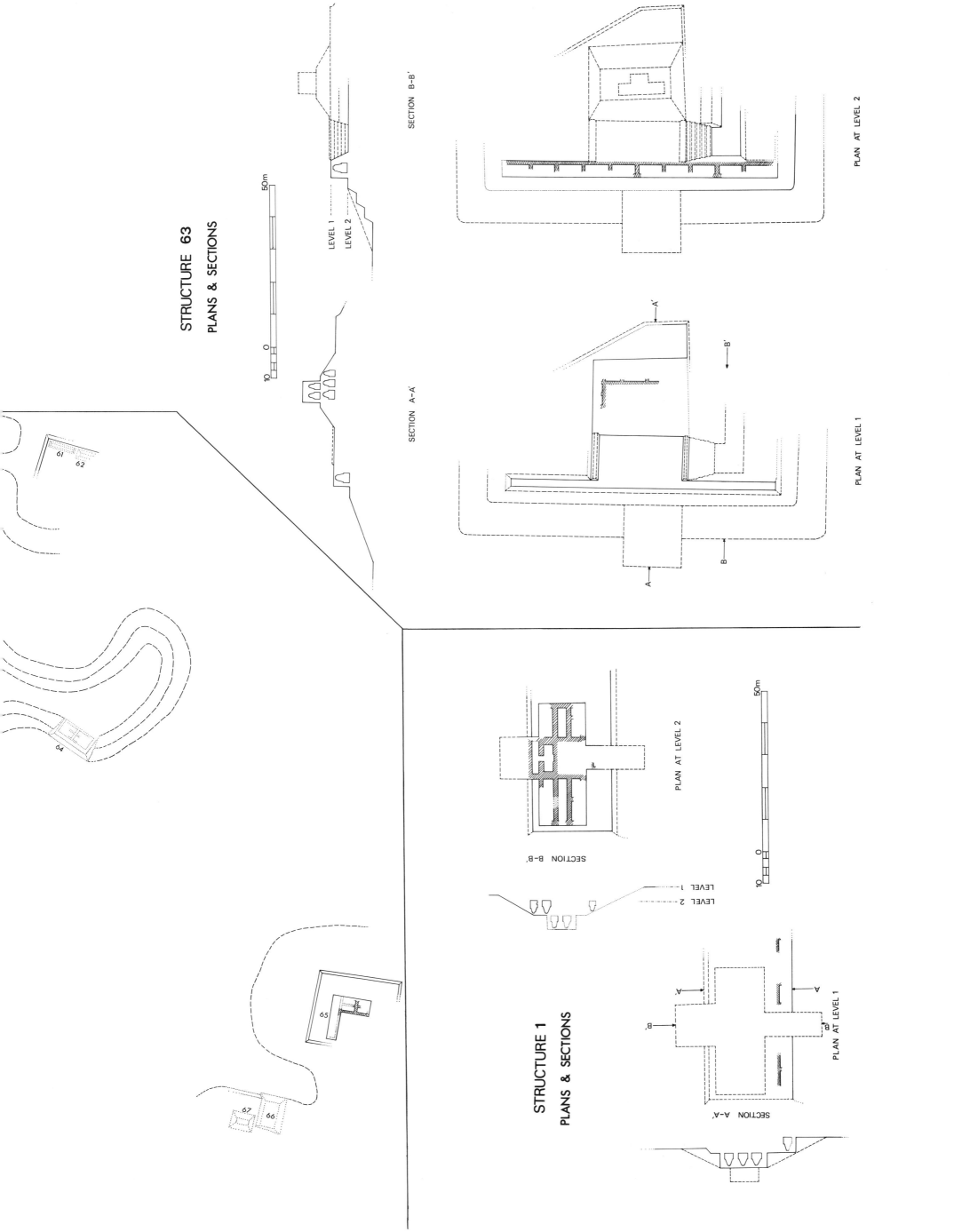

STRUCTURE 63
PLANS & SECTIONS

SECTION B-B'

LEVEL 1
LEVEL 2

PLAN AT LEVEL 2

50m

0

10

SECTION A-A'

PLAN AT LEVEL 1

61

62

64

65

66

67

STRUCTURE 1
PLANS & SECTIONS

PLAN AT LEVEL 2

SECTION B-B'

LEVEL 1
LEVEL 2

50m

0

10

PLAN AT LEVEL 1

SECTION A-A'

reaching a maximum height of 22 m, is the highest structure in Itzimte.

All the stelae at the site were found on the low platform designated as Structure 30. When the stelae were first seen several pieces had been overturned and the fragments were in obvious disarray. It was apparent that looting had occurred and even though a thorough search for the missing fragments was made, many never appeared. It is not only the looters that can be held accountable for the destruction of the sculpture, the burning of the fields in preparation for planting has not only obliterated the details of sculpture exposed to the fire, but has damaged even those pieces which fell face down, the high temperature cracking the stone.

In addition to the pieces published here, some small fragments were found and photographed. Little detail is left in them and as it could not be determined from which stela they had broken off, they have not been included here, but can nevertheless be found in the archives of the Peabody Museum.

When Stephens was at the site, it was already known as Itzimte (he spelled it Ytsimpte). The name has consequently been retained (as Itzimte-Bolonchen), even though there is another site with inscriptions by that name in Guatemala, usually spelled Itsimte, however.

REGISTER OF INSCRIPTIONS AT ITZIMTE

Stelae 1 and 3 to 12
(Stela 2 is plain)
Lintel 1

REFERENCES CITED

MALER, TEOBERT
    1902   "Yukatekische Forschungen," *Globus*, vol. 82, pp. 216-217.

RUZ LHUILLIER, ALBERTO
    1945   "Campeche en la Arqueología Maya," *Acta Anthropologica* I:2-3, p. 47.

STEPHENS, JOHN LLOYD
    1848   *Incidents of Travel in Yucatan*, vol. 2, pp. 139-141. Harper and Bros., New York.

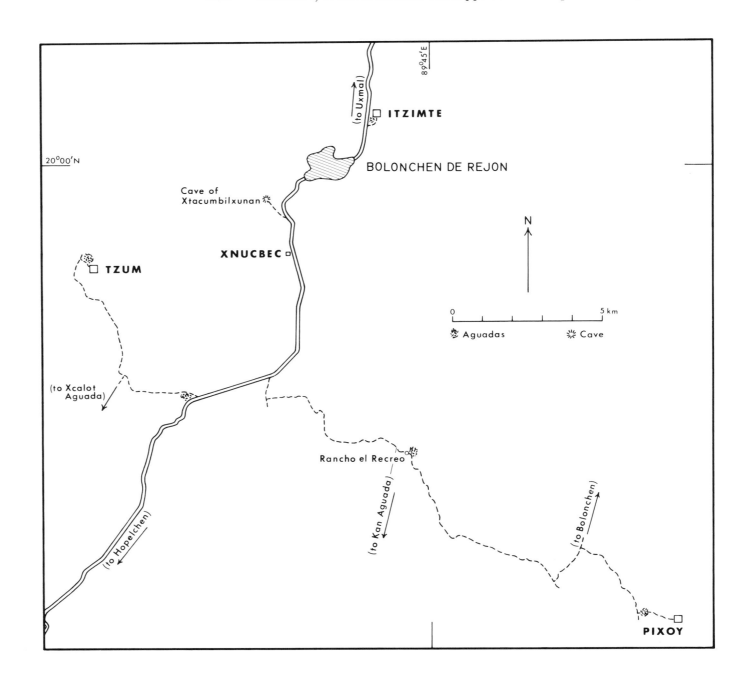

Itzimte, Stela 1

LOCATION Westernmost of the twelve stelae set up on Structure 30, the stela platform. It was taken to the Campeche Museum in 1973.

CONDITION The lower piece was found in situ, but was almost completely calcined by fire. The main portion of the stela was lying face down in front of the butt, well preserved but broken into many pieces. Several small fragments were not found.

MATERIAL Limestone.

SHAPE Parallel sides. Shape of top unknown.

DIMENSIONS
HLC	2.15 m (estimated)
PB	Unknown
MW	0.90 m
WBC	0.90 m
MTh	0.33 m
Rel	3.7 cm

CARVED AREAS Front only.

PHOTOGRAPHS von Euw.

DRAWING von Euw, based on field drawing corrected by artificial light.

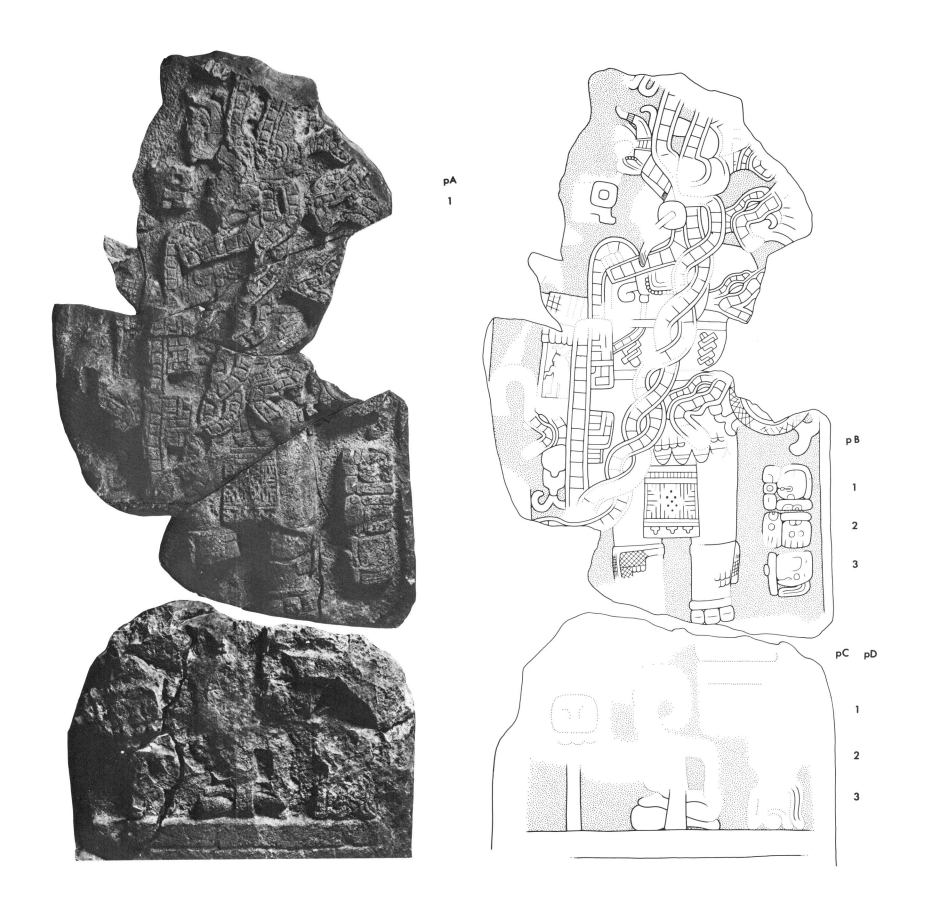

Itzimte, Stela 3

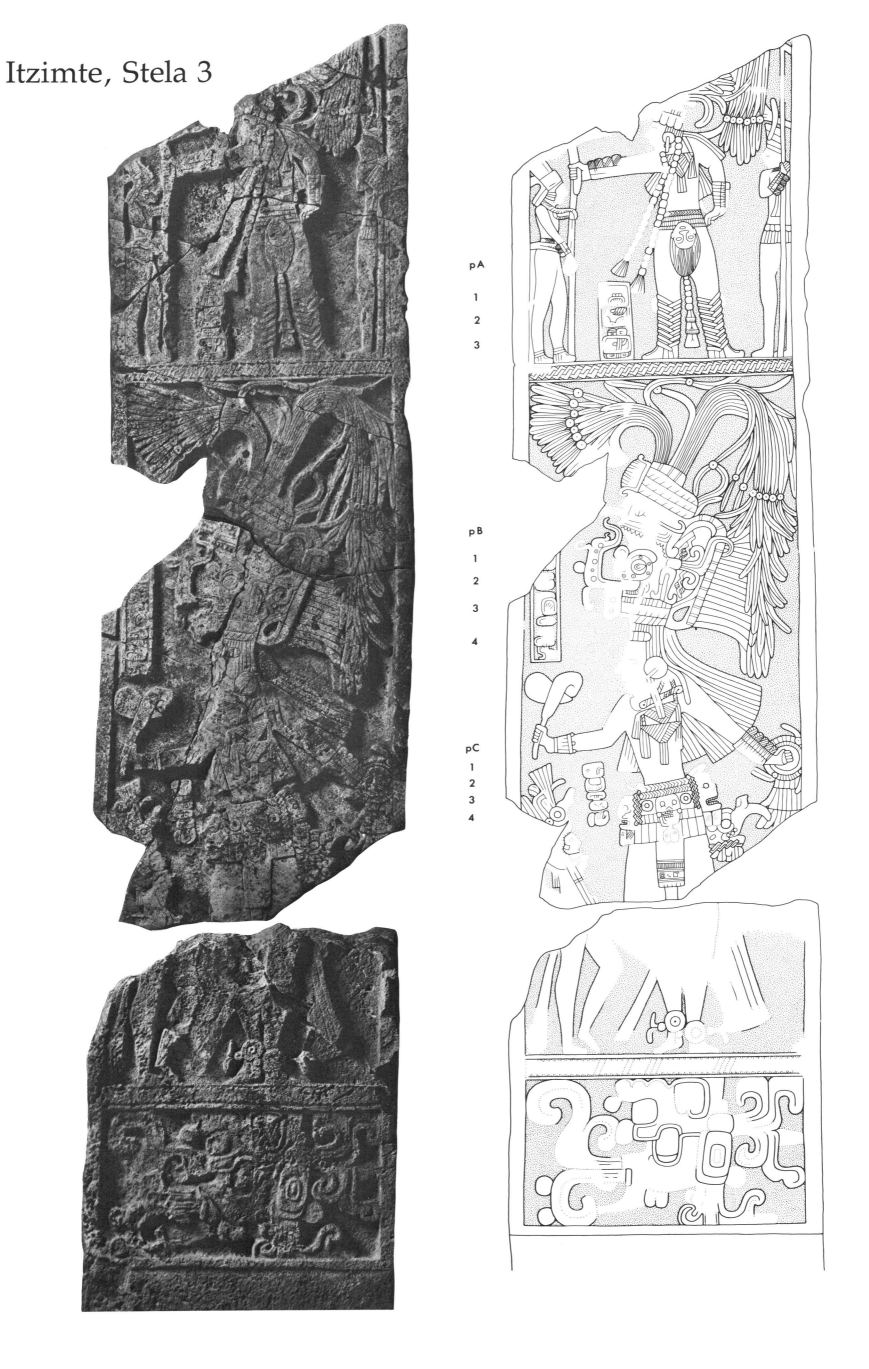

pA
1
2
3

pB
1
2
3
4

pC
1
2
3
4

LOCATION On Structure 30, between Stelae 2 and 4. It was removed to the Campeche Museum in 1973.

CONDITION The lower fragment was found standing erect in place, but the sculptured surface had been severely burned, and most of the detail has been lost. The rest of the stela was found broken into many pieces (obviously cracked by the heat of the fire to which it had been exposed), but was nevertheless excellently preserved. Several fragments were missing.

MATERIAL Limestone.

SHAPE Long thin shaft with parallel sides. Form of top unknown

DIMENSIONS HLC 3.30 m (estimated)
PB 0.77 m
MW 0.83 m
WBC 0.83 m
MTh 0.33 m
Rel 2.7 cm

CARVED AREAS Front only.

PHOTOGRAPHS von Euw.

DRAWING von Euw, based on field drawing corrected by artificial light.

Itzimte, Stela 4

LOCATION It was found lying approximately halfway between Stelae 3 and 5 on Structure 30. Taken to the Campeche Museum in 1973.

CONDITION Cracked into many pieces, several of which (including the butt) have been lost. The degree of preservation varies greatly depending on the severity of the exposure to fire.

MATERIAL Limestone.

SHAPE Parallel sides, with rounded or triangular top.

DIMENSIONS
H   2.00 m (estimated height of surviving fragments)
MW   1.24 m
MTh 0.22 m
Rel 1.8 cm

CARVED AREAS Front only.

PHOTOGRAPHS von Euw.

DRAWING von Euw, based on field drawing corrected by artificial light.

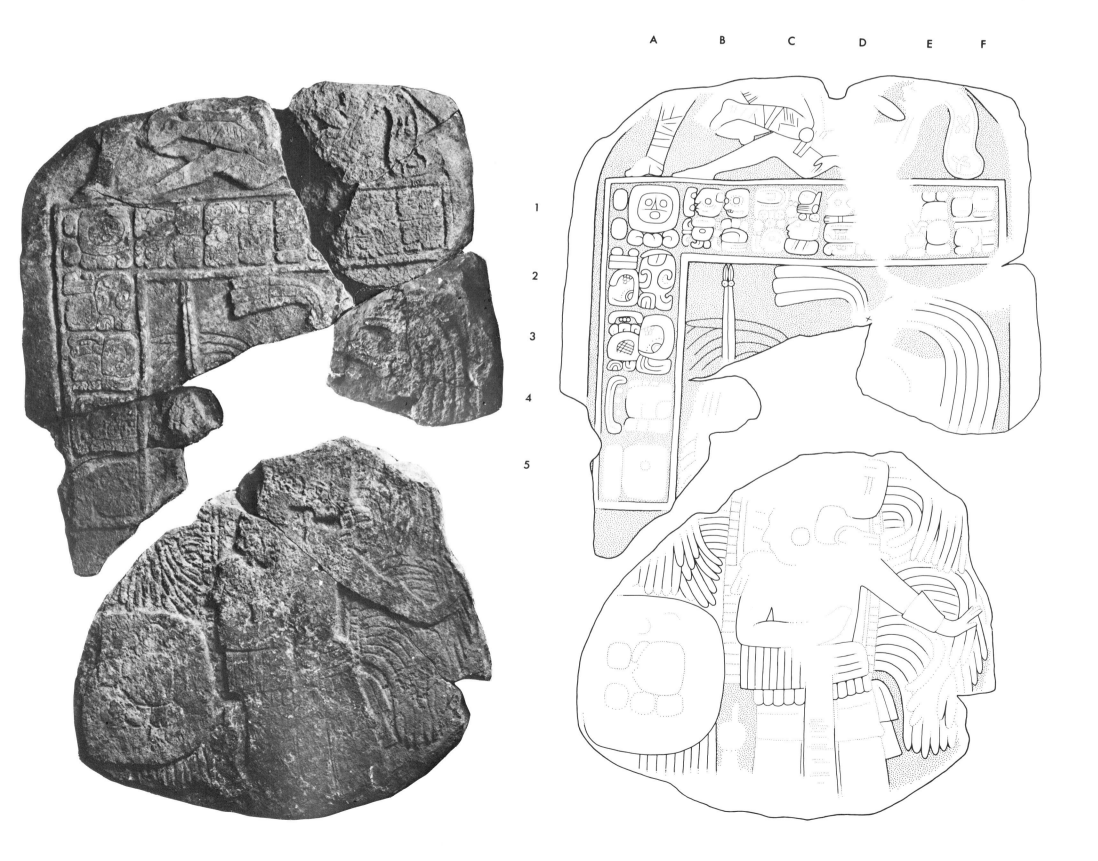

Itzimte, Stela 5

LOCATION The base of the stela was found in situ approximately aligned with (and between) Stelae 3 and 7 on Structure 30. It was taken to the Campeche Museum in 1973.

CONDITION Broken in many pieces. Where the sculptured area was exposed to fire, calcination was extensive; otherwise the preservation was very good. A large portion of the stela was not found.

MATERIAL Limestone

SHAPE Parallel sides, with rounded top.

DIMENSIONS H 2.56 m (height of fragment)
MW 0.95 m
MTh 0.36 m
Rel 3.0 cm

CARVED AREAS Front only.

PHOTOGRAPHS von Euw.

DRAWING von Euw, based on field drawing corrected by artificial light.

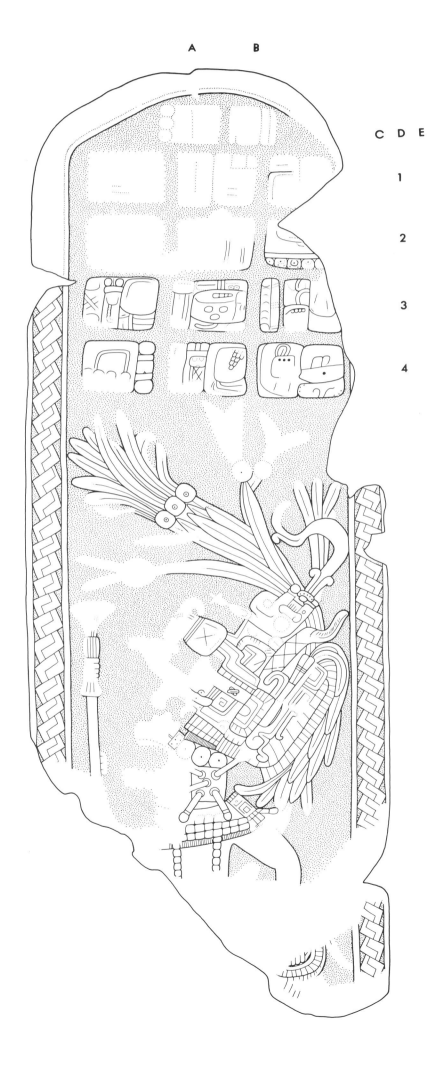

Itzimte, Stela 6

LOCATION On the stela platform, Structure 30. It was found lying between Stelae 5 and 7, although not aligned with them; the butt was not buried. In 1973 the stela was removed to the Campeche Museum.

CONDITION In two pieces. Slight erosion in the upper one, but considerable loss in detail due to fire in the lower fragment.

MATERIAL Limestone.

SHAPE Parallel sides with flattish, rounded top.

DIMENSIONS HLC   1.32 m
               PB   0.24 m
               MW   0.82 m
               WBC   0.80 m
               MTh   0.25 m
               Rel   1.2 cm

CARVED AREAS Front only.

PHOTOGRAPH von Euw.

DRAWING von Euw, based on field drawing corrected by artificial light.

Itzimte, Stela 7

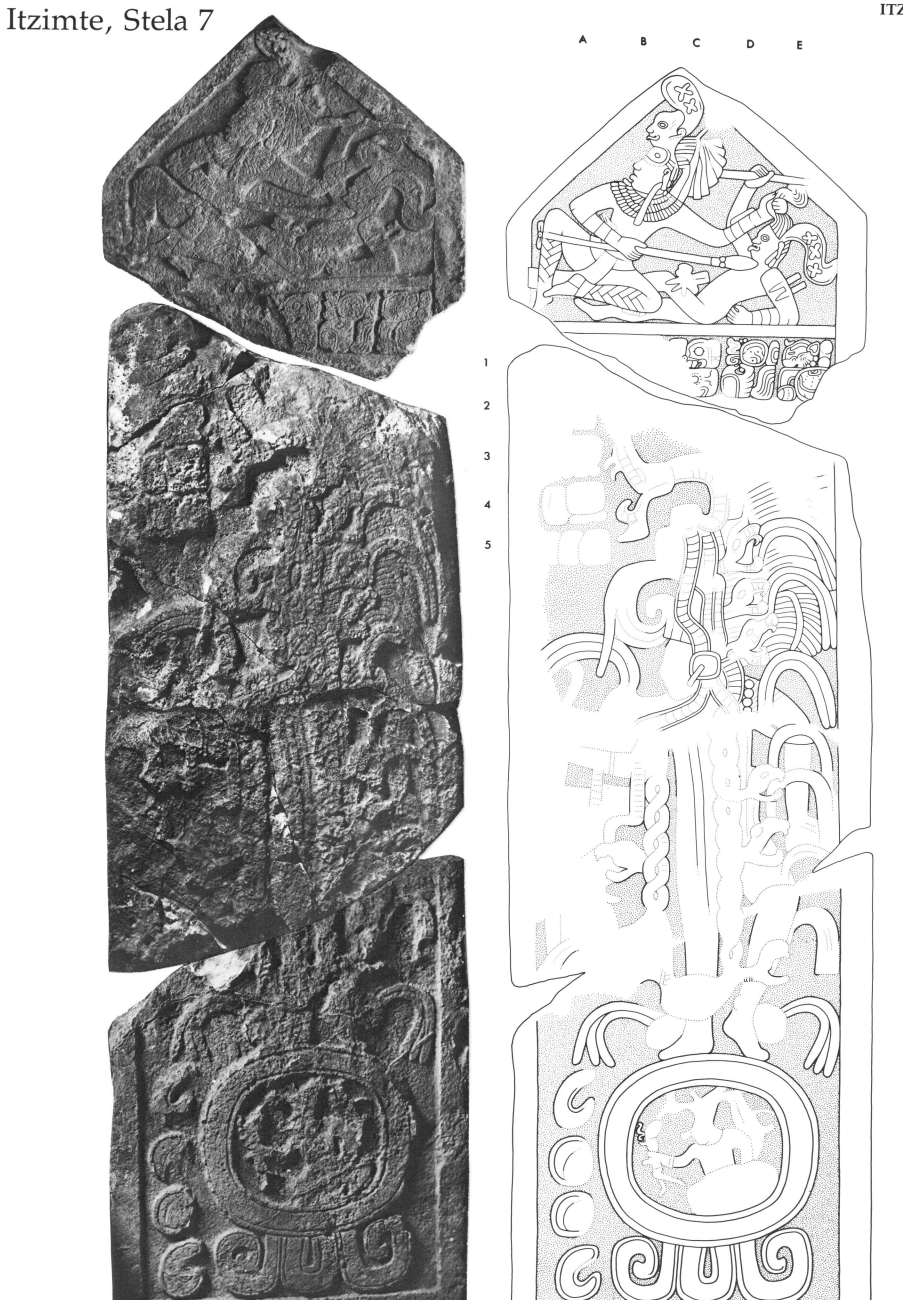

LOCATION The lower fragment was found standing in place between the bases of Stelae 5 and 8 (although closer to 8) on Structure 30. It was removed with other fragments to the Campeche Museum in 1973. The upper fragment is in a private collection in Mexico City.

CONDITION Except for the piece in Mexico City, the stela was in a rather friable state because of exposure to fire.

MATERIAL Limestone.

SHAPE Long thin shaft with parallel sides and a triangular top.

DIMENSIONS HLC 3.40 m
PB Not measured
MW 0.95 m
WBC 0.94 m
MTh 0.27 m
Rel 2.7 cm

CARVED AREAS Front only.

PHOTOGRAPHS von Euw.

DRAWING von Euw, based on field drawing corrected by artificial light.

Itzimte, Stela 8

LOCATION Between Stelae 7 and 9 on Structure 30. Removed in 1973 to the Campeche Museum.

CONDITION Found in many severely burned pieces; the detail has been almost completely lost by calcination. Several fragments were missing.

MATERIAL Limestone.

SHAPE Parallel sides. Form of top unknown

DIMENSIONS HLC 1.82 m (estimated)
PB   Not measured
MW   0.72 m
MTh   0.35 m
Rel   2.2 cm

CARVED AREAS Front only.

PHOTOGRAPHS von Euw, except upper right fragment of the base which was photographed by Anthony P. Andrews in 1976.

DRAWING von Euw, based on field drawing corrected by artificial light.

A

p1

2

3

4

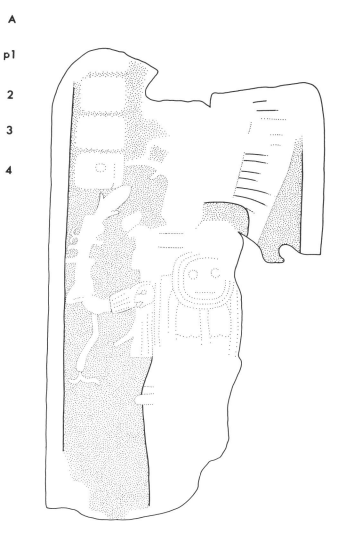

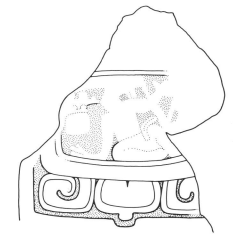

LOCATION   The butt of the stela was found
in situ 2.5 m east of Stela 8 on Structure 30.
The main fragments of Stelae 9 and 10 were
found somewhat distant from their bases.
Because the dimensions of these fragments
are fairly similar and because each one is
consistent with the dimensions and
carving of the butt of Stela 9, it is unclear
which one is in fact a part of this stela and
which one is a part of Stela 10. With some
misgivings, but not without reason (see
ITZ: St. 10), the relation of the large
fragments to the butts was assumed.

CONDITION   The main fragment has
suffered from erosion and some burning,
and the lower fragments have been badly
calcined. Several pieces were not found
and are assumed to have been looted or
burned beyond recognition.

MATERIAL   Limestone.

SHAPE   Parallel sides with a triangular top.

DIMENSIONS   HLC   2.80 m (estimated)
             PB   Not measured
             MW   0.87 m
             WBC   0.87 m
             MTh   0.24 m
             Rel   2.4 cm

CARVED AREAS   Front only.

PHOTOGRAPHS   von Euw, except for the
small upper left fragment of the base which
was photographed by Agustín Peña in
1976.

DRAWING   von Euw, based on field
drawing corrected by artificial light.

Itzimte, Stela 10

LOCATION The main fragment was found several meters away from the butt, which was found in situ approximately 3 m east of Stela 9, making it the easternmost surely placed monument on Structure 30. Because of similarities in style it seems probable that the small fragment with the foot carved on it is a part of the same stela as the larger piece. The butt of Stela 9 has carving, while that of Stela 10 shows none and as the "foot" fragment is apparently the lowest piece of a stela, it could be a part of Stela 10 but not of Stela 9. It was in view of this that the correspondence of the large fragments and the butts was assumed.

CONDITION In three pieces, although the butt was not photographed; all fragments have lost details through erosion.

MATERIAL Limestone.

SHAPE Parallel sides; shape of top unknown.

DIMENSIONS
HLC	1.46 m (estimated)	
PB	Not measured	
MW	0.91 m	
WBC	0.91 m	
MTh	0.27 m	
Rel	1.5 cm	

CARVED AREAS Front only.

PHOTOGRAPHS von Euw.

DRAWING von Euw, based on field drawing corrected by artificial light.

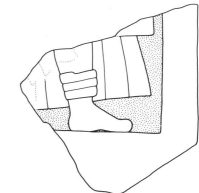

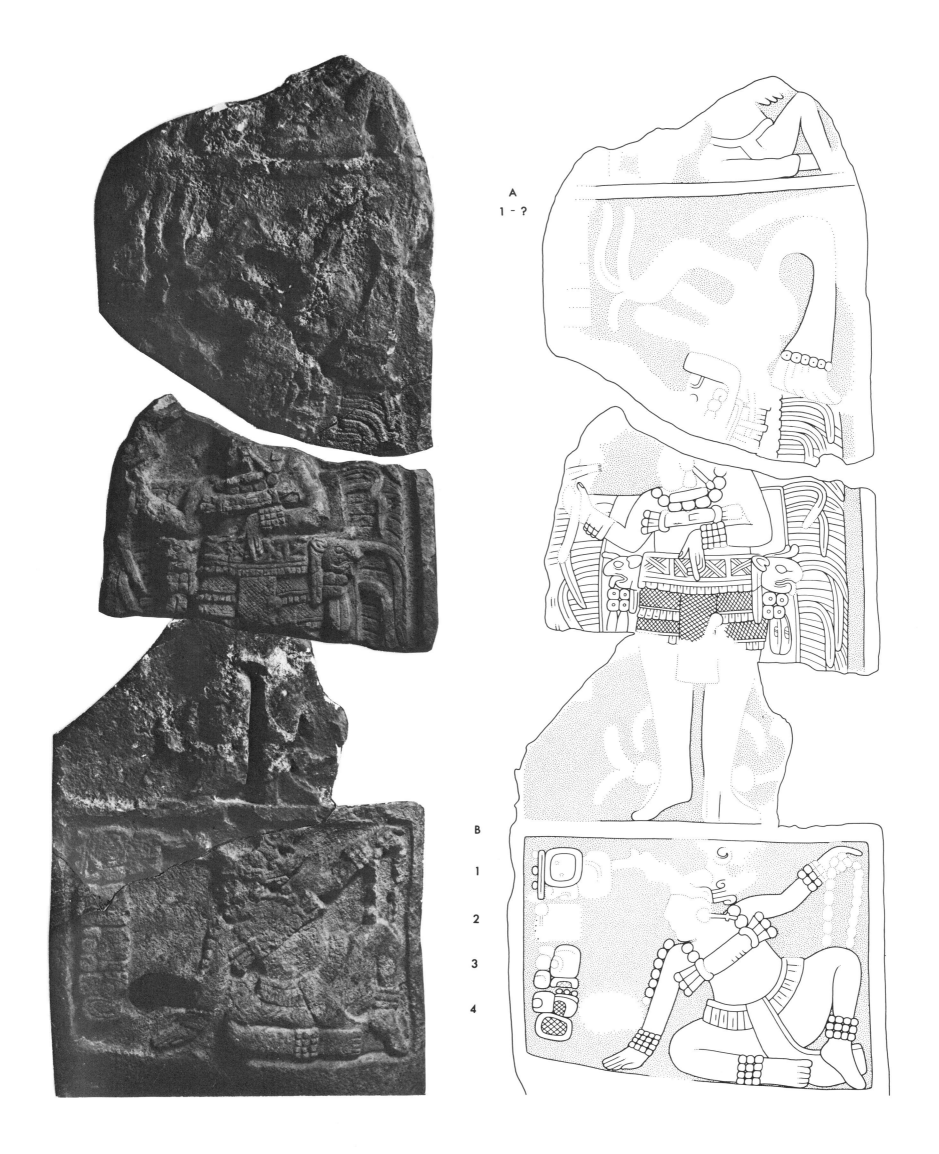

A
1 - ?

B

1

2

3

4

LOCATION Easternmost of the monuments on Structure 30. The butt of the stela was no longer set in the ground, and the fragments were found scattered near Stela 10. It was removed in 1973 to the Campeche Museum.

CONDITION As is the case with other sculpture on this stela platform, the condition of this stela varies greatly with the degree of exposure to fire: from a well preserved middle fragment to a badly calcined upper piece. Several small fragments were not found.

MATERIAL Limestone.

SHAPE Parallel sides. Form of top unknown.

DIMENSIONS

HLC	2.72 m
PB	0.20 m
MW	0.99 m
WBC	0.99 m
MTh	0.30 m
Rel	3.5 cm

CARVED AREAS Front only.

PHOTOGRAPHS von Euw, except for the small piece on the lower right of the top fragment which was photographed by Norberto Gonzalez Crespo in 1976.

DRAWING von Euw, based on field drawing corrected by artificial light.

Itzimte, Stela 12

LOCATION It was found lying under a large fragment of Stela 3. Removed to the Campeche Museum in 1973.

CONDITION In two pieces, the stela has suffered from erosion and, especially on the sides, from calcination.

MATERIAL Limestone.

SHAPE Almost square. An unusually small standing monument.

DIMENSIONS
HLC	0.51 m	
PB	0.02 m	
MW	0.55 m	
MTh	0.24 m	
Rel	1.1 cm	

CARVED AREAS Front, sides, and top.

PHOTOGRAPHS von Euw.

DRAWINGS von Euw, based on field drawings corrected by artificial light.

Front

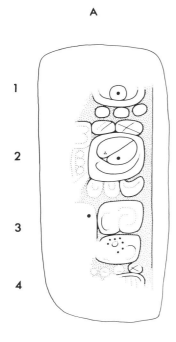

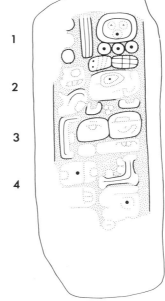

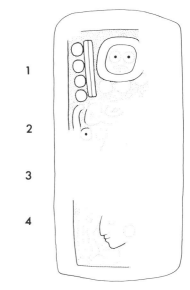

Left side

Top

Right side

Itzimte, Lintel 1

LOCATION Found in the debris of Structure 39. Taken in 1973 to the Campeche Museum.

CONDITION Found in four pieces. Portions of the front and the underside have been lost. The sculptured surface on the underside is in excellent condition, while the inscription in the front is somewhat eroded.

MATERIAL Limestone.

SHAPE Parallel sides with irregular extremes.

DIMENSIONS
Lintel:

	H	0.27 m
	MW	0.68 m
	MTh	1.50 m
Sculptured area (under-side):		
	H	1.26 m
	MW	0.62 m
	Rel	2.0 cm

CARVED AREAS Front and underside.

PHOTOGRAPHS von Euw.

DRAWINGS von Euw, based on field drawings corrected by artificial light.

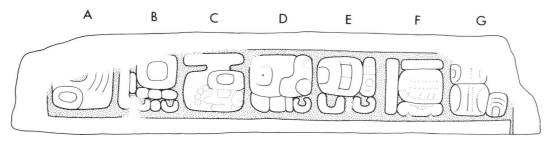

Front

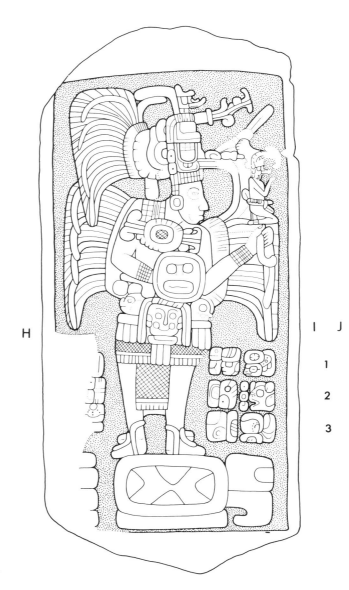

Underside

Pixoy

LOCATION AND ACCESS

Pixoy is located on a hilltop 19.5 km southeast of Bolonchen, Campeche. It is possible to drive to within approximately 1 km of the site. One must first drive south from the town on the Bolonchen-Hopelchen highway for 8 km, then turn south into a dirt road, which one soon leaves to take the road to the ranch of Don Octavio Ramírez (Rancho el Recreo). Continuing in a generally southeasterly direction for about 6.5 km, one reaches an extensive savanna (in which many *pixoy* trees are growing), and then proceeds along hilly terrain for 2 km until coming to an *aguada*—the *aguada* Pixoy or Pixoy Akal. This is a very unreliable source of water, and it was completely dry during my visit to the site (Don Octavio, who has an apiary nearby, supplied us with several drums of water for our stay). From the *aguada*, Pixoy is reached by walking uphill due east for about 1 km. The ruins are located in land belonging to the Ejido de Bolonchen.

PRINCIPAL INVESTIGATIONS AT THE SITE

The site had been visited previously only by looters, who left many holes and sherds in their wake. The register of the sculpture and the map were produced during two visits totaling 11 days in 1973. In 1974 a brief visit to the site was made by E. Wyllys Andrews V, of Tulane University.

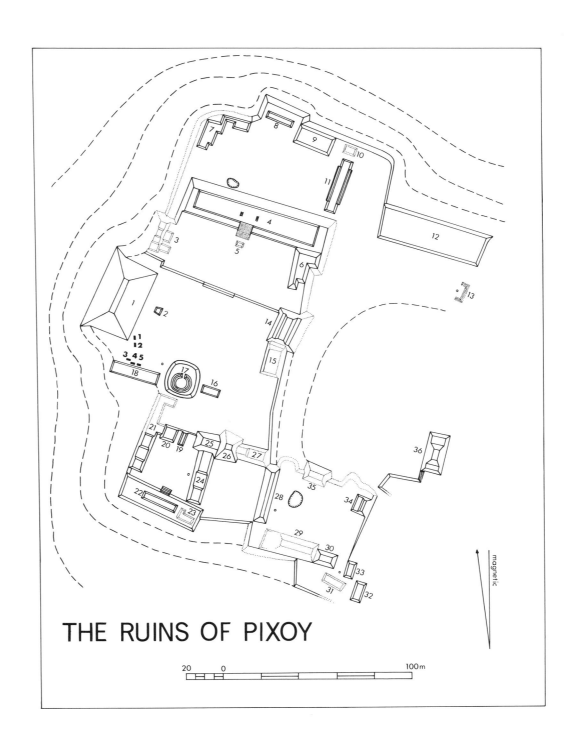

THE RUINS OF PIXOY

NOTES ON THE RUINS

The exact orientation of the stelae (except Stela 4) is unknown, as they were apparently moved during the looting. It seems reasonable, however, that they were originally placed near Structure 18.

Pixoy is a small site with only two structures higher than 10 m. Structure 1 is the highest at the site (12 m), but the two-storied Structure 4 seems to have been the most important. The lower level is formed by three rows of rooms, the front two generally connected (except when directly below or adjacent to the staircase). Only the rooms on the east and west extremes are oriented in a north-south direction. The second story has almost completely collapsed.

The entrance to Structure 22 has a well preserved stone mask above the lintel. This mask has several portions covered by stucco and red paint. Red paint can also be found clinging to parts of a mat design carved on a column altar between Structures 11 and 12.

On a capstone in Structure 15 (PIX: Msc. 1) there are traces of painted glyphs, but unfortunately most of the surface has been lost to erosion.

A portion of a carved figure in very deep relief was found in front of Structure 1. Unfortunately only the mid-section of the figure was found (showing the belt with hanging heads and shells, and the remains of the lower arm).

REGISTER OF INSCRIPTIONS AT PIXOY

Stelae 1 to 5
Miscellaneous 1

Pixoy, Stela 1

LOCATION The three fragments of the stela were found scattered near the southeastern corner of Structure 1.

CONDITION The stela is broken into three large pieces, all of which are somewhat weathered. It is, nevertheless, the best preserved stela at the site.

MATERIAL Limestone.

SHAPE Parallel sides tapering asymmetrically to a rounded top.

DIMENSIONS HLC 2.47 m (estimated)
PB 0.57 m
MW 0.90 m
WBC 0.90 m
MTh 0.33 m
Rel 2.3 cm

CARVED AREAS Front only.

PHOTOGRAPHS von Euw.

DRAWING von Euw, based on field drawing corrected by artificial light.

Pixoy, Stela 2

LOCATION Found scattered in several pieces near the southeastern corner of Structure 1. Original orientation unknown.

CONDITION In three fragments, all very eroded.

MATERIAL Limestone.

SHAPE Parallel sides with an asymmetrically rounded top.

DIMENSIONS
HLC 2.50 (estimated)
PB 0.76 m
MW 0.90 m
WBC 0.85 m
MTh 0.36 m
Rel 0.8 cm

CARVED AREAS Front only.

PHOTOGRAPHS von Euw.

DRAWING von Euw, based on field drawing corrected by artificial light.

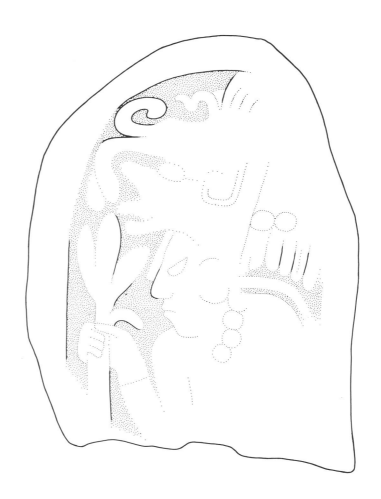

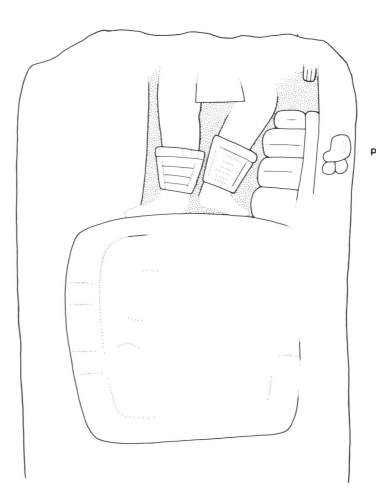

pA

Pixoy, Stela 3

LOCATION Found lying face up near Stela 4, between Structures 1 and 18, though somewhat closer to the latter.

CONDITION Only one fragment was found and it is in very poor condition. The top half of the stela is missing.

MATERIAL Limestone.

SHAPE The width increases from bottom to top. The carved surface is slightly convex.

DIMENSIONS
HLC 1.30 m (fragment)
PB 0.23 m
MW 1.10 m
WBC Unknown
MTh 0.38 m
Rel 1.1 cm

CARVED AREAS Front only.

PHOTOGRAPH von Euw.

DRAWING von Euw, based on field drawing corrected by artificial light.

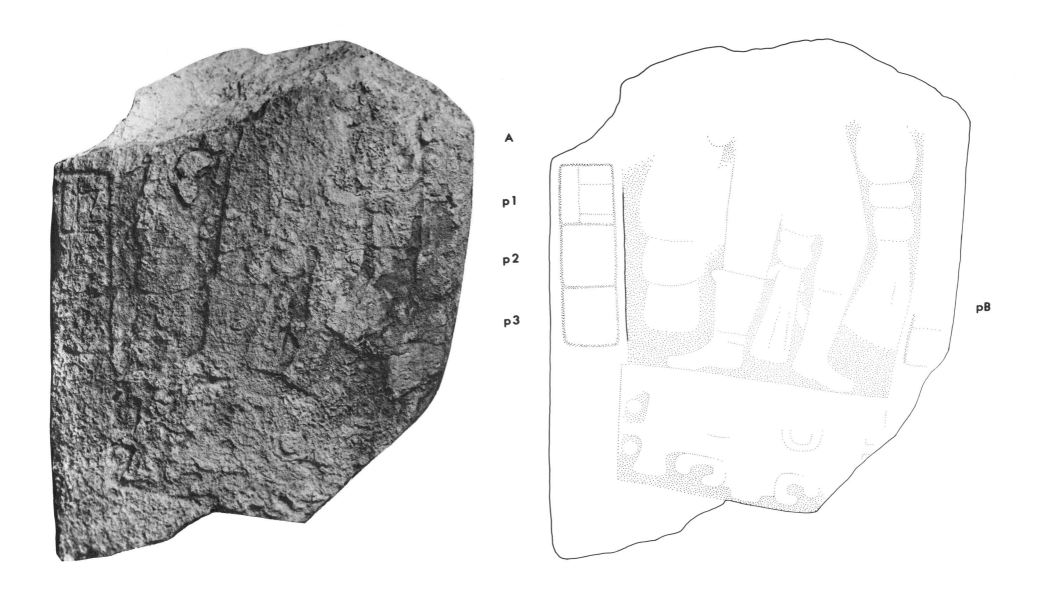

A

p1

p2

p3

pB

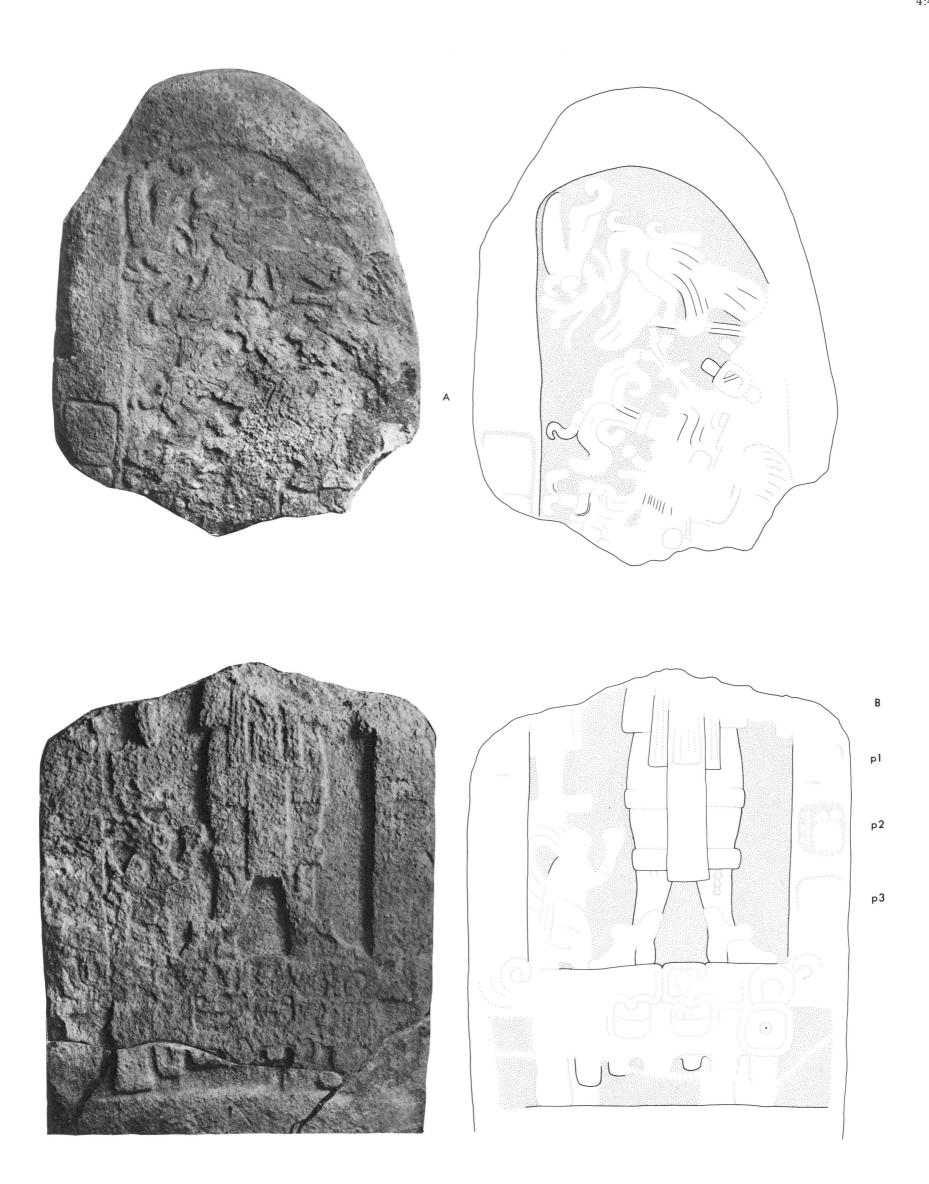

LOCATION   The butt of the stela was found in situ in front of Structure 18 (the only monument found in place), with the bottom fragment lying face up nearby. The top fragment had fallen or was thrown into a hole about 2 m deep from where it was lifted with considerable difficulty.

CONDITION   All three fragments are in rather eroded condition, and pieces are obviously missing.

MATERIAL   Limestone.

SHAPE   Generally parallel sides topped off by an irregularly rounded top.

DIMENSIONS   HLC   2.75 m (estimated)
PB   Unknown
MW   1.01 m
WBC   1.00 m
MTh   0.30 m
Rel   3.0 cm

CARVED AREAS   Front only.

PHOTOGRAPHS   von Euw.

DRAWING   von Euw, based on field drawing corrected by artificial light.

Pixoy, Stela 5

LOCATION Found scattered east of Stela 4, near Structure 18. It had apparently been moved from its original placement by looters.

CONDITION The stela was found in what seemed to be two large pieces, but the condition of the stone was quite friable and several fragments came loose with handling.

MATERIAL Limestone.

SHAPE Parallel sides. Form of top unknown.

DIMENSIONS
HLC 2.06 m
PB 0.21 m
MW 0.64 m
WBC Unknown
MTh 0.24 m
Rel 1.2 cm

CARVED AREAS Front only.

PHOTOGRAPHS von Euw.

DRAWING von Euw, based on field drawing corrected by artificial light.

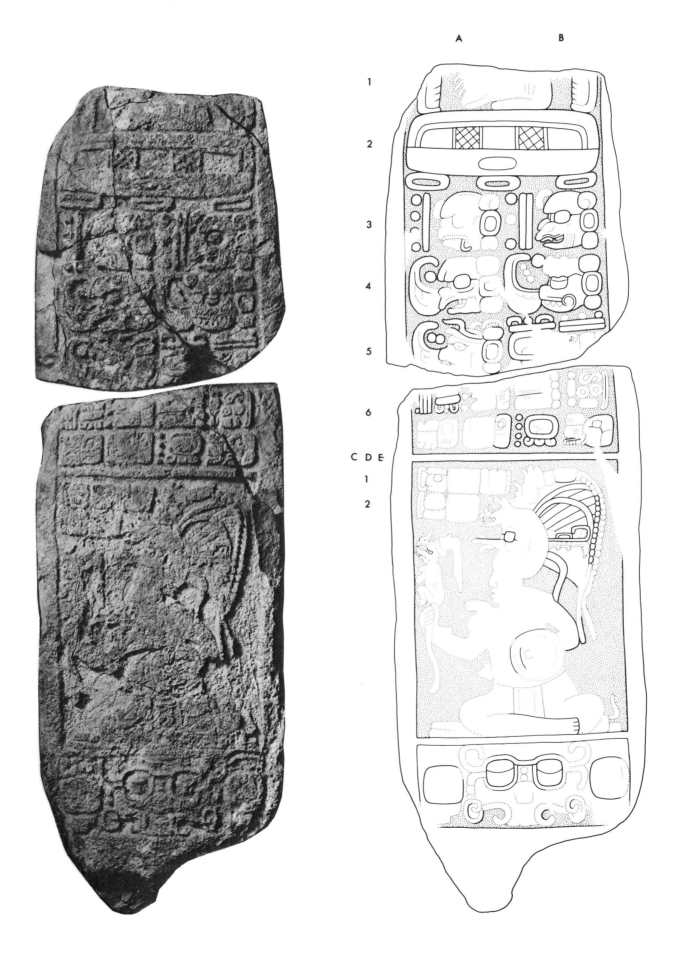

Pixoy, Miscellaneous 1

LOCATION Structure 15 is almost completely collapsed, but the capstone (Miscellaneous 1) is still visible in it.

CONDITION Only faint traces of the glyphs remain.

MATERIAL Red paint on plaster-covered limestone.

DIMENSIONS H 0.59 m (Exposed area only. The capstone is embedded in mortar for about 0.30 m on each end.)
MW 0.43 m
MTh 0.28 m

PAINTED AREAS Underside only.

PHOTOGRAPH E. Wyllys Andrews V.

Tzum

LOCATION AND ACCESS

Although Tzum is only 8.5 km west southwest from Bolonchen de Rejón, the easiest route to the ruins is much more circuitous. One takes the paved road south from Bolonchen for about 11.5 km, turning west at the turnoff for Kinin along a dirt road. Soon one passes an *aguada* (which contained water during the 1975 season) and continues in a westerly direction for about 2.5 km and then for a short distance in a northwesterly direction until a fork is reached. Taking the right-hand road (the other goes to Xcalot, 3 km away) one continues in a generally northwesterly direction through rather flat, low growth or *milpa* country for about 5 km when one goes off into a *milpa* road in a southeasterly direction for about 300 m until reaching the *aguada* (dry in 1975), which is a couple of hundred meters from the site.

PRINCIPAL INVESTIGATIONS AT THE SITE

The information presented here was obtained in visits totaling 14 days in May and June of 1975. No previous work (except for looting depredation) had been carried out at the site.

NOTES ON THE RUINS

The site is formed by five fairly well defined groups (all but one on hilltops) connected by a series of *sacbes*.

There is a ball court in Group A (Structures A-45, 46) located south of the largest structure at the site (A-21). Structure A-21 has several well preserved (though looted) rooms and is 11 m at its highest point.

All the stelae and Miscellaneous Sculptures 1-15 were found in Group B. Considerable looting has taken place, leaving fragments of the same monument separated by as much as 12 m and, as a consequence, the location of the stelae is merely conjectural. It is quite probable that many of the missing fragments have been looted, as a careful search for them was unsuccessful. Structure B-2 dominates this group rising to a height of 10.5 m.

Other large structures are C-3, D-2, E-3, and E-2 with heights of 6.5, 10.5, 9, and 6.8 m respectively. D-2 also has several rooms that are still standing.

The *sacbes* are mostly very low, reaching a maximum height of about only 2 m between Groups C and D.

North of Structure C-1, the top half of a figure was found, carved almost in the round, but it was extremely eroded and was not photographed.

REGISTER OF INSCRIPTIONS AT TZUM

Stelae 1 to 6
Sculptured stones 1 to 15

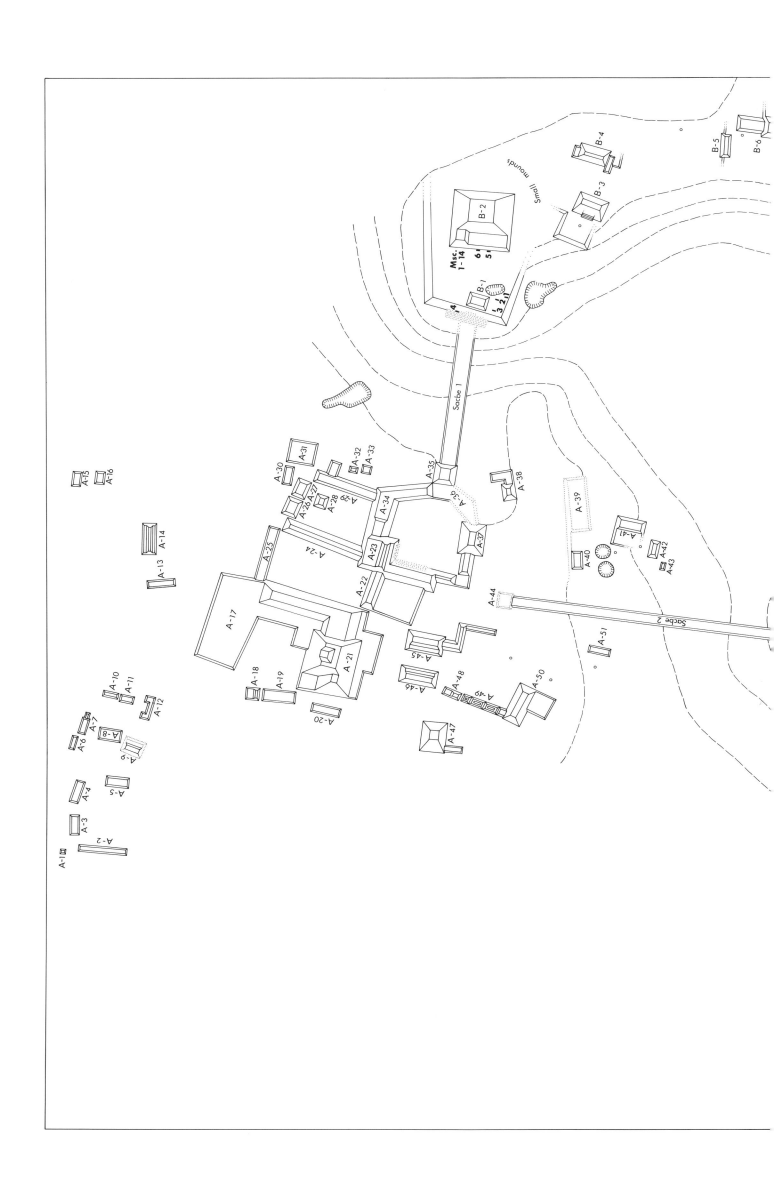

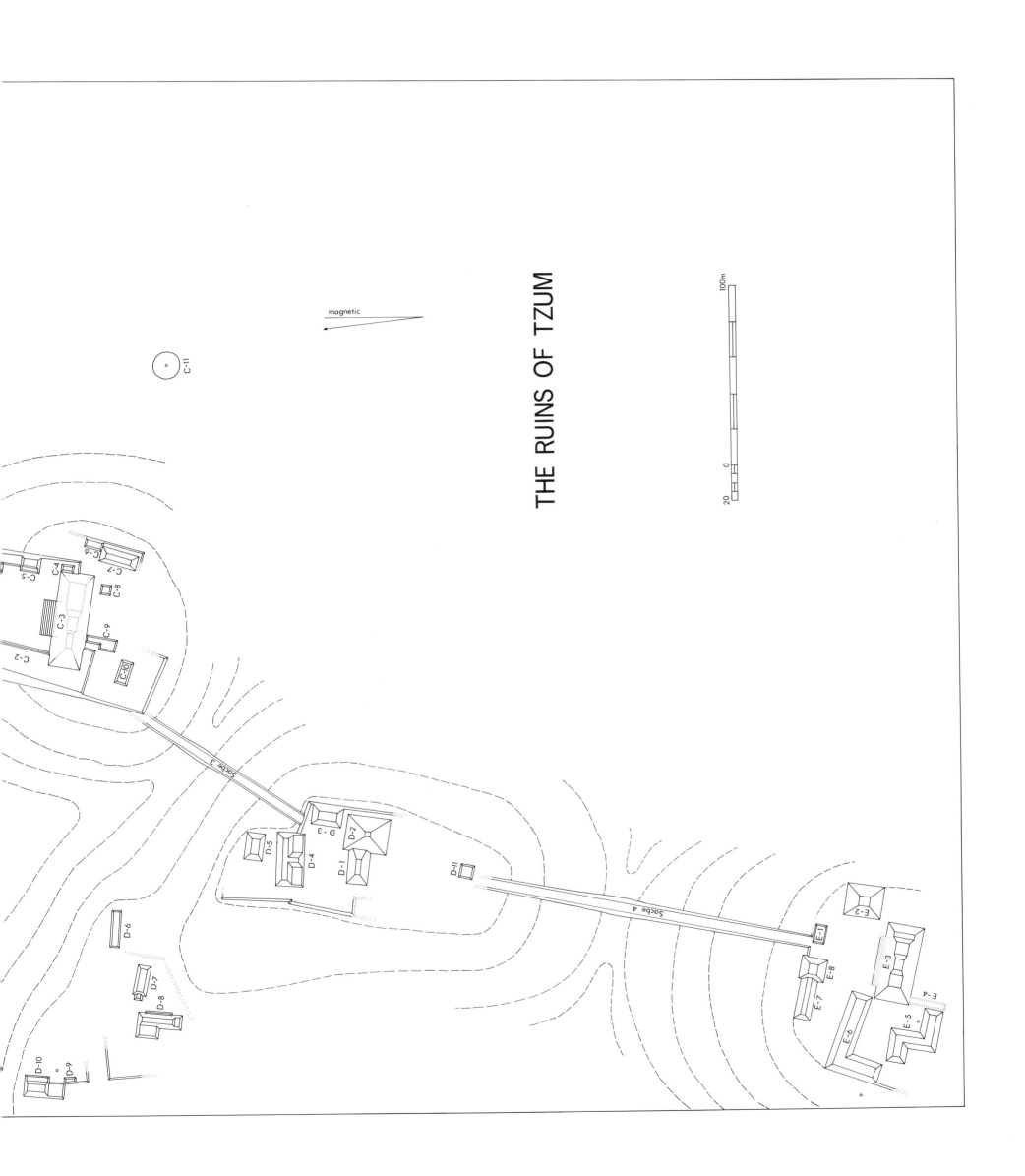

THE RUINS OF TZUM

magnetic

100m

20   0

C-11

Tzum, Stela 1

Back

Front

pE   pF   pG   pH

1·2

3

4

5

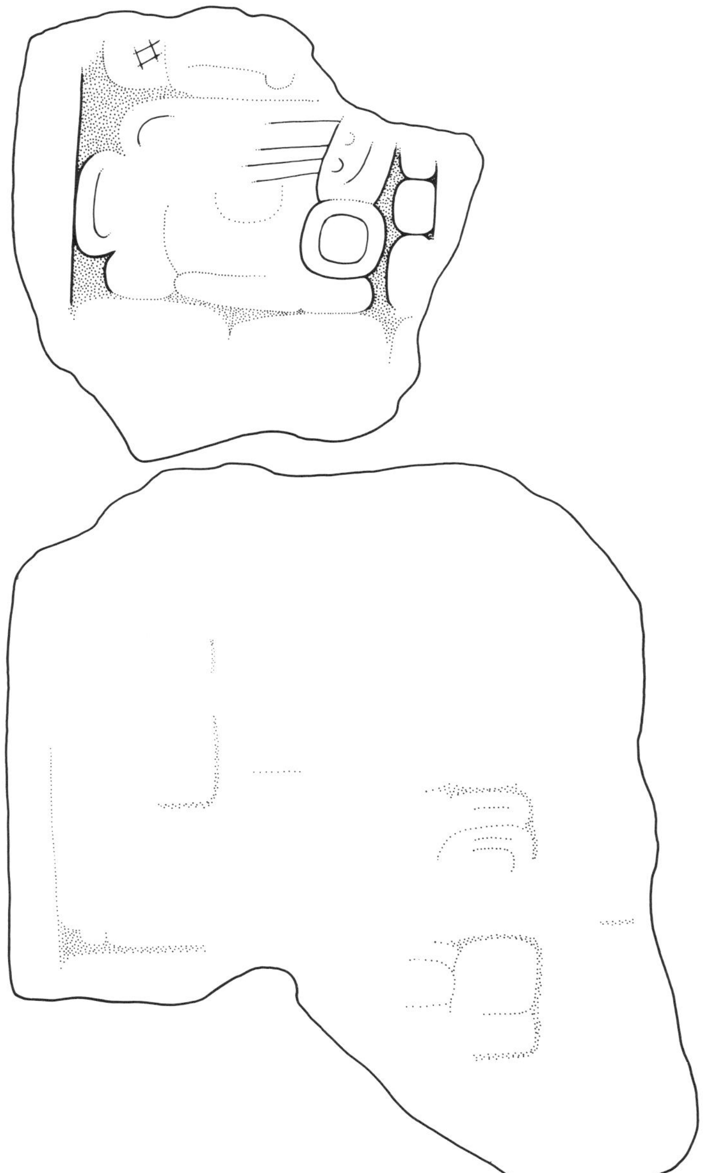

pA

1

2

pB

1

2

3

4

LOCATION The fragments were found widely separated from each other south of Structure B-1; they had obviously been moved and their original position could not be ascertained.

CONDITION The main group of fragments was found scattered over an area of about six square meters. Although much detail remains, the stone is quite friable as the result of fires. A saw cut is also in evidence. The two other fragments, found about 10 or 12 m away, are perhaps in worse condition. Most of this stela has probably been removed by looters.

MATERIAL Limestone with iron oxide veins.

SHAPE Parallel sides; shape of top unknown.

DIMENSIONS HLC 1.70 m (estimated from surviving fragments)
PB 0.14 m plus
MW 0.96 m
MTh 0.33 m
Rel 2.0 cm

CARVED AREAS Front, back, and sides.

PHOTOGRAPHS von Euw.

DRAWINGS von Euw, based on field drawings corrected by artificial light.

pC
1
2

pD
1
2
3

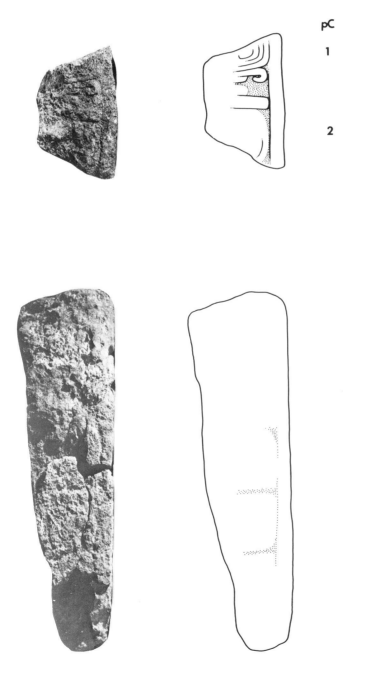

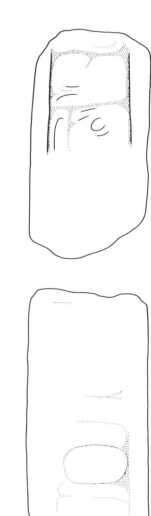

Left side

Right side

Tzum, Stela 2

LOCATION   South of Structure B-1.

CONDITION   The right side of the stela somehow survived burning and is in very good condition, although the other surfaces are pitted and eroded. The top and bottom fragments have disappeared.

MATERIAL   Limestone with iron oxide veins.

SHAPE   Parallel sides; shape of top unknown.

DIMENSIONS   HLC   1.28 m
            PB   Unknown
            MW   0.88 m
            WBC   Unknown
            MTh   0.33 m
            Rel   2.0 cm

CARVED AREAS   Front and sides.

PHOTOGRAPHS   von Euw.

DRAWINGS   von Euw, based on field drawings corrected by artificial light.

pA

Front

Left side

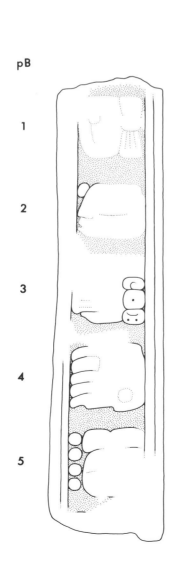

pB

1

2

3

4

5

Right side

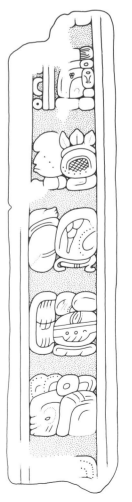

pC

1

2

3

4

5

6

7

Tzum, Stela 3

LOCATION South of Structure B-1.

CONDITION Several pieces are missing. Some have been sawed off, others are presumed to have been taken by looters. The many fragments were found scattered over a large area. In general the pieces are in good condition, although they have been damaged by burning. The right side is completely eroded.

MATERIAL Limestone with iron oxide veins.

SHAPE Sides seem to be tapering off to a rounded top.

DIMENSIONS
HLC	2.40 m
PB	0.14 m
MW	0.90 m
WBC	Unknown
MTh	0.43 m
Rel	1.8 cm

CARVED AREAS Front and sides.

PHOTOGRAPHS von Euw.

DRAWINGS von Euw, based on field drawings corrected by artificial light.

Front

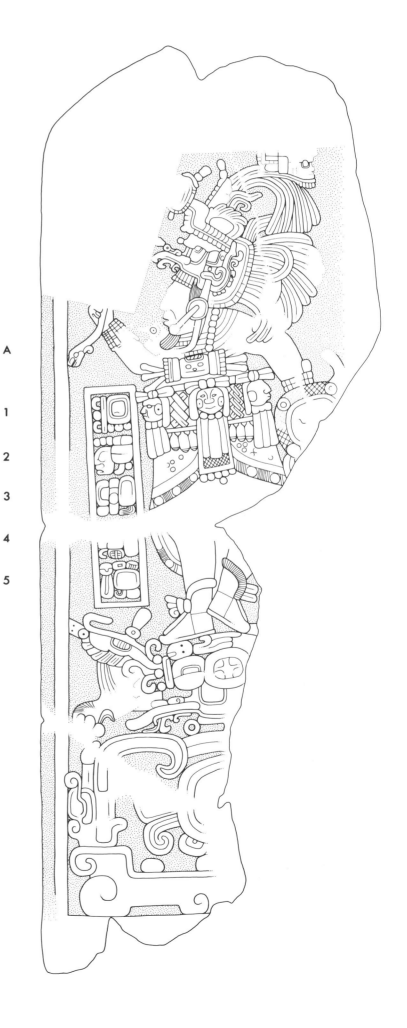

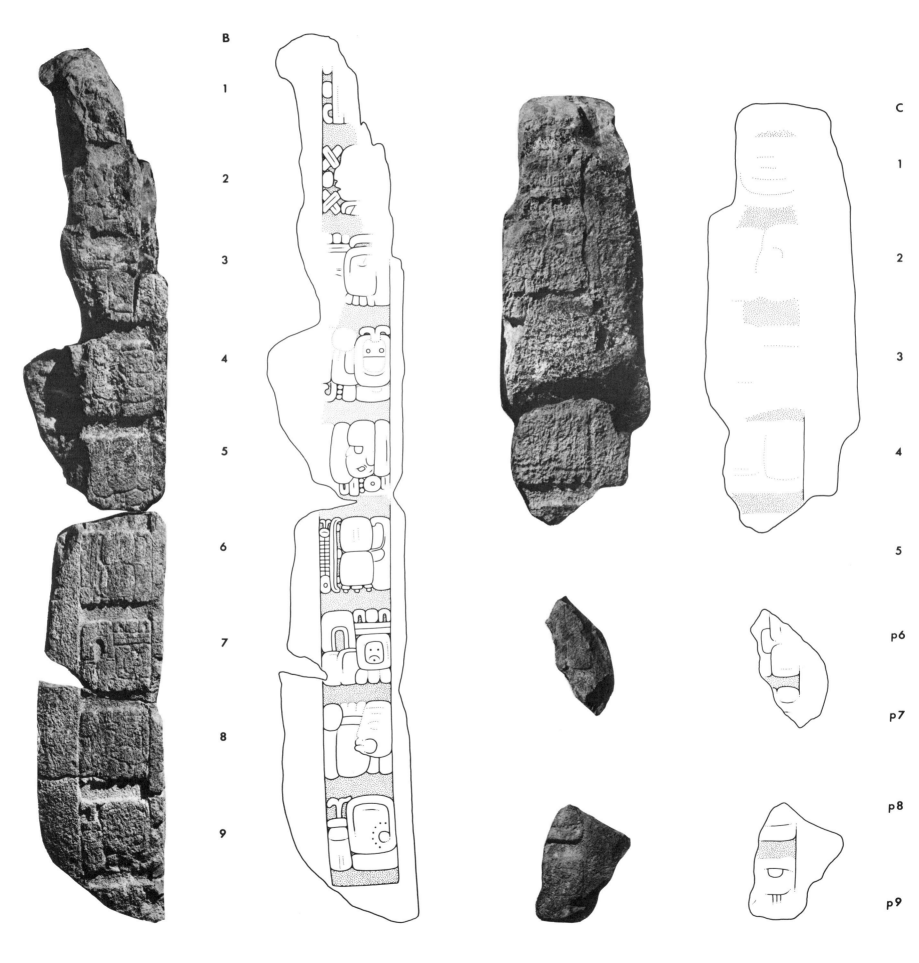

Left side   *Right side*

Tzum, Stela 4

LOCATION The fragments were found on the stairway leading to the platform serving as a base to Structures B-1 and B-2.

CONDITION Three large fragments were found, but large portions of the stela are missing. The condition, except for a small area on the front surface, is very poor, and the sides show little more than outlines of glyphs.

MATERIAL Limestone with iron oxide veins. Perhaps somewhat more porous than other monuments at the site.

SHAPE Sides fairly parallel; shape of top unknown.

DIMENSIONS
HLC	1.93 m
PB	0.58 m
MW	0.96 m
WBC	0.95 m
MTh	0.31 m
Rel	1.5 cm

CARVED AREAS Front and sides.

PHOTOGRAPHS von Euw.

DRAWINGS von Euw, based on field drawings corrected by artificial light.

Front

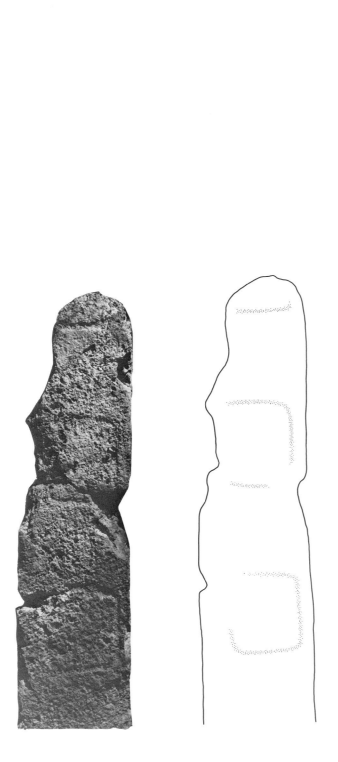

Left side

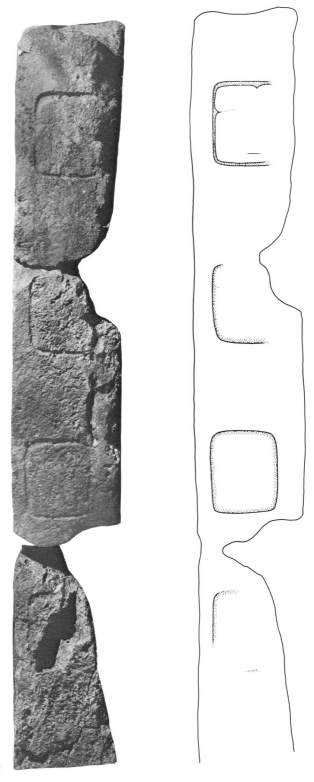

Right side

Tzum, Stela 5

LOCATION Found near the base of the platform leading to Structure B-2, on its western extreme.

CONDITION A great deal of weathering as well as some burning has left the stela in a rather fragile state. Many fragments are missing even though a day-long search for them was undertaken, and they are presumed to have been calcined beyond recognition.

MATERIAL Limestone with iron oxide veins.

SHAPE Sides taper off to a rounded top.

DIMENSIONS
HLC	1.50 m (estimated)
PB	0.54 m
MW	0.60 m
WBC	Unknown
MTh	0.39 m
Rel	1.5 cm

CARVED AREAS Front and sides.

PHOTOGRAPHS von Euw.

DRAWINGS von Euw, based on field drawings corrected by artificial light.

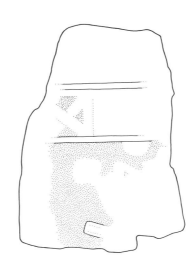

pA

1

2

Front

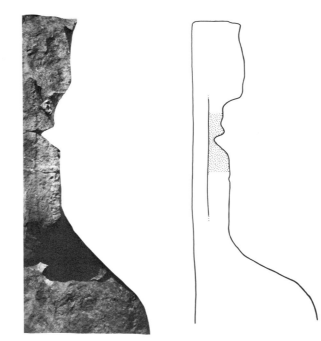

Left side

Right side

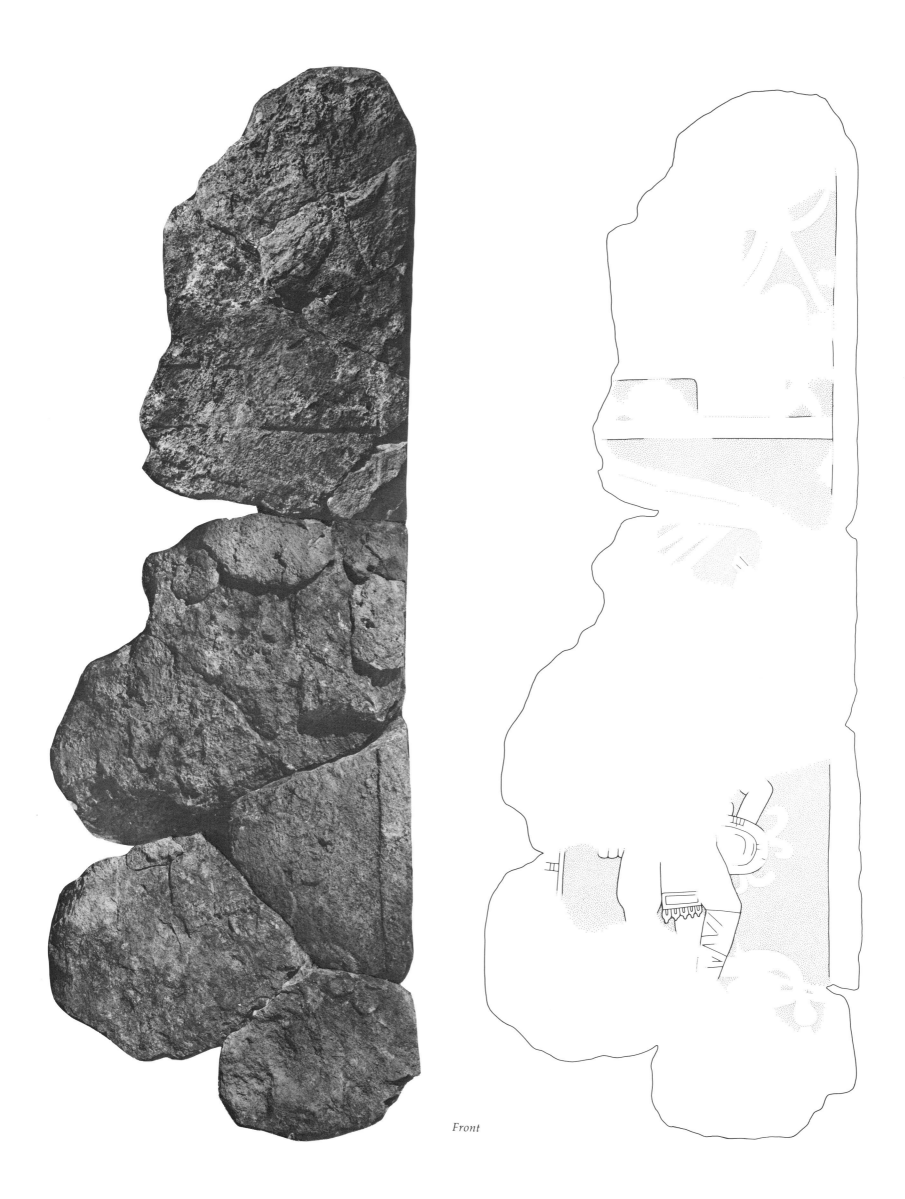

Front

LOCATION On platform leading to Structure B-1, just north of Stela 5.

CONDITION Except for a few areas (notably the right side) the stela has suffered greatly from burning and erosion, and only small areas contain recognizable carving. Much of the stela is missing.

MATERIAL Limestone.

SHAPE Probably had parallel sides; shape of top unknown.

DIMENSIONS MH 2.86 m (estimated)
MW 1.03 m
MTh 0.52 m
Rel 1.0 cm (front)
1.5 cm (back)
1.3 cm (sides, except for the circular holes in the right side, whose relief is 3.0 cm)

CARVED AREAS Front, back, and sides.

PHOTOGRAPHS von Euw.

DRAWINGS von Euw, based on field drawings corrected by artificial light.

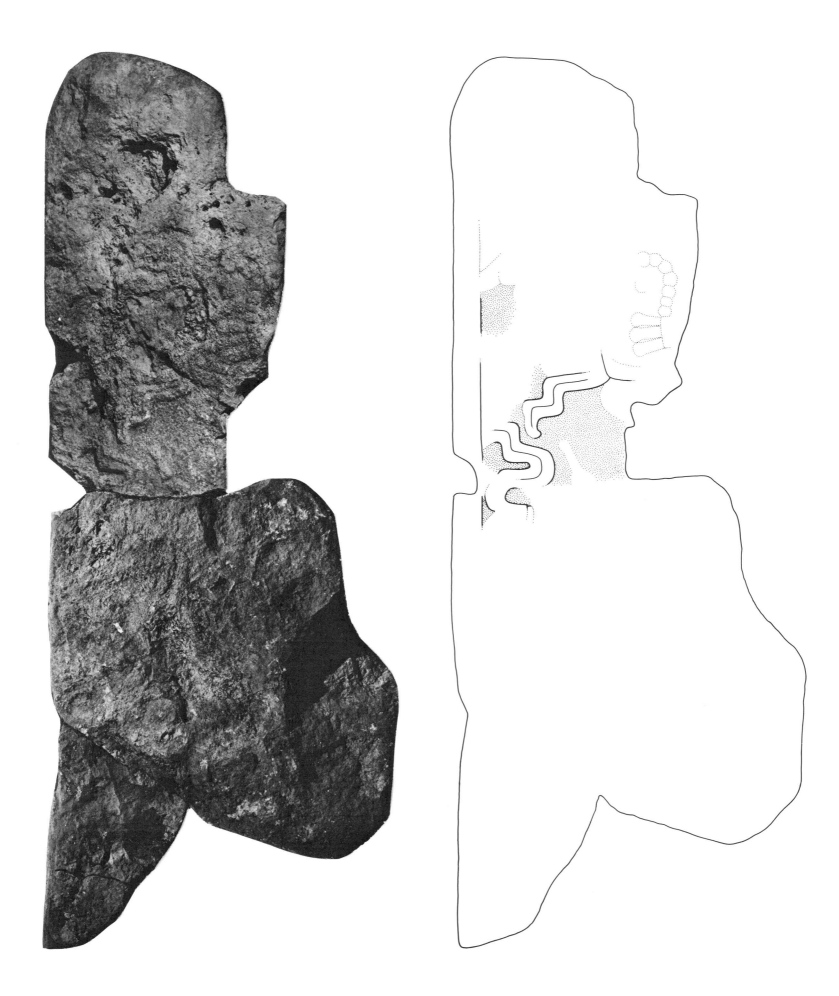

Back

Left side

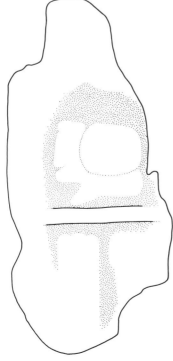

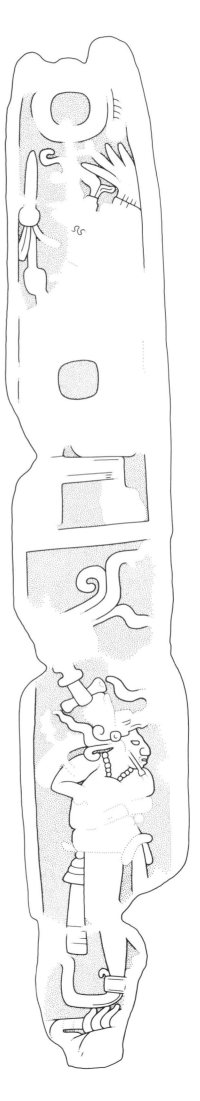

Right side

Tzum, Miscellaneous Sculptures 1-15

LOCATION Stones 1-14 were found lying scattered west of the northwestern extension of Structure B-2, just off the platform. Stone 15 had been thrown into the cave southeast of Structure B-1.

CONDITION All stones are quite weathered. Stones 9 and 15 are each in two pieces.

MATERIAL Limestone.

SHAPE Stones 1-14 are rectangular, most of them nearly square. Stone 15 has been sawn and its shape is therefore unknown.

DIMENSIONS All dimensions are given in centimeters.

Stone	1	2	3	4	5
H	29.5	29.0	28.0	30.0	28.0
W	33.5	29.0	26.0	33.0	29.0
Th	17.0	18.0	28.0	20.0	19.0
Rel	0.4	0.4	0.5	0.5	0.4

Stone	6	7	8	9	10
H	29.0	29.0	31.0	29.0	35.0
W	34.0	27.5	32.0	29.0	28.0
Th	22.0	22.0	19.0	28.0	26.0
Rel	0.4	0.5	0.4	0.4	0.4

Stone	11	12	13	14	15
H	28.0	30.0	30.0	29.0	19.0
W	28.0	29.0	33.0	32.0	57.0
Th	17.0	17.0	15.0	21.0	
Rel	0.4	0.4	0.4	0.4	

CARVED AREAS Stones 3 and 9 are each carved on two adjacent sides. All others are carved on one surface only.

PHOTOGRAPHS von Euw.

DRAWINGS von Euw, based on field drawings corrected by artificial light, except Stone 15, which was based on photographs only.

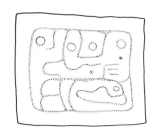

1

2

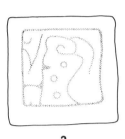

3a

3b

4

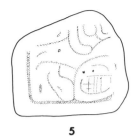 

5

6

7

8

9a

9b

10

11

12

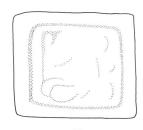

13

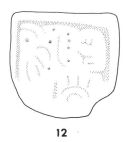

14

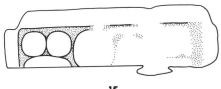

15